AMAZING
BASKETBALL
STORIES FOR KIDS

*Unforgettable Hoops Heroes and
Inspiring Moments That Will Ignite
Your Love for Basketball*

LEIGH JORDYN

TABLE OF CONTENTS

BEN WALLACE

INTRODUCTION

Hello, young readers! I'm Leigh Jordyn, and I'm here to share some incredible stories that I think you will enjoy. You see, I'm not just an author; I'm also a mom to three incredible boys who share a passion for sports, especially basketball. Our home is often filled with the sound of bouncing balls and the excitement of watching NBA games on TV with their dad. As I watched their eyes light up with every dunk, every three-pointer, and every fast break, I was reminded of the magic that basketball brings to our lives.

That's why I decided to write "Amazing Basketball Stories for Kids." This book isn't just about the game itself; it's about the stories behind the players who have inspired my boys and countless other kids around the world. As parents, we want our children, YOU, to be surrounded by positive influences, and what better way to do that than through the stories of basketball legends?

Basketball is more than just a sport; it's a journey of hard work, dedication, and determination. When I look at basketball athletes like Michael Jordan, LeBron James, Stephen Curry, and Giannis Antetokounmpo, I see more than just players on the court. I see individuals who have transformed their dreams into reality, and that's a lesson I want my boys – and all young readers – to take to heart.

Through these remarkable athletes, we learn that basketball is a vessel for valuable life lessons and values. Perseverance, teamwork, leadership, and giving back are all integral parts of the game and qualities that can guide us in our own lives.

My goal with "Amazing Basketball Stories for Kids" is simple: I want to inspire young readers to dream big, work hard, and believe in themselves. As you flip through the pages of this book, I hope you'll find not just stories of basketball, but stories of resilience, courage, and the power of the human spirit. Whether you're on the court or off, these stories will remind you that every journey begins with a single step, and every dream is within reach.

So, let's lace up our imaginary sneakers, dribble through challenges, and shoot for the stars. Let the stories of these incredible basketball athletes guide you as you chase your own hoop dreams. After all, the game of life is the greatest adventure, and with determination and passion, you can make every moment count!

MICHAEL JORDAN

"Obstacles don't have to stop you. If you run into a wall, don't turn around and give up. Figure out how to climb it, go through it, or work around it."
- Michael Jordan

In the world of basketball, one name shines brighter than the rest – Michael Jordan. This is the incredible true story of a boy who turned his dreams into reality and became a basketball superstar loved by people all around the world. So, grab your basketball and get ready to be inspired by the remarkable journey of Michael Jordan!

From the moment Michael was a little kid, he couldn't get enough of basketball. He dribbled and shot hoops in his backyard for hours, rain or shine. His love for the game was like a spark that kept growing brighter and brighter, guiding him through every challenge.

When Michael was in high school, he had a dream to play basketball on the school team. He practiced endlessly, honing his skills and perfecting his shots. He was excited to try out for the team, believing that his hard work would pay off.

But the day of the tryouts arrived, and things didn't go as planned. The coaches had to make difficult choices, and Michael's name wasn't on the list of players who made the team. He felt a mix of disappointment and frustration. It was a tough moment for him, and he could have easily given up on his dream right then and there.

However, Michael was not the kind of person to back down easily. Instead of letting the disappointment get the best of him, he decided to turn it into fuel for his determination. He made a promise to himself that he would work harder than ever before. He saw this setback as a challenge that he was determined to overcome. *"Whenever I was working out and got tired and figured I ought to stop, I'd close my eyes and see that list in the locker room without my name on it,"* Jordan said, *"and that usually got me going again."*

From that day on, Michael's life revolved around basketball even more intensely. He woke up early in the morning and practiced before school. After classes, he would head to the court and keep practicing until the sun went down. He dribbled, shot, and practiced every move he could think of. His friends and family often saw him dribbling a basketball wherever he went – in the hallway, in the backyard, and even in his room!

People around him began to notice the incredible dedication he was putting into improving his skills. They could see the fire in his eyes, the determination that was driving him forward. Michael wasn't just practicing; he was pouring his heart and soul into the game he loved.

Michael's hard work and dedication didn't go unnoticed for long. The next year, when the tryouts came around again, he was ready. He had transformed himself into a better player, someone who was more skilled, focused, and confident. The coaches saw his improvement and determination, and this time, his name was proudly announced as a member of the basketball team.

But Michael didn't stop there. He knew that making the team wasn't the end of the journey; it was just the beginning. He continued to work harder than ever, pushing himself to improve even more. He wasn't satisfied with just being on the team; he wanted to be a leader, someone who could inspire and guide his teammates.

And that's exactly what he did. With Michael's dedication and leadership, the team began to shine. They practiced together, learned from each other, and grew stronger as a unit. They won games and faced challenges with a newfound resilience. Michael's passion and perseverance were contagious, inspiring his teammates to give their all.

Before long, Michael was not only a member of the team but also its leader. He led them to victories and became a role model for everyone around him. His journey from disappointment to triumph showed that setbacks can be stepping stones to success, and hard work can turn dreams into reality.

As he grew older, Michael's dedication to basketball only got stronger. He played in college and then got a chance to join the NBA with the Chicago Bulls. But being good wasn't enough for Michael. He wanted to be great! So, he practiced tirelessly, pushing himself to jump higher, run faster, and shoot more accurately. He knew that dreams don't just come true; you have to chase them with all your might.

When Michael stepped onto the basketball court, it was like magic. He leaped through the air with grace, scoring points that seemed impossible. People everywhere cheered for him, and they called him "Air Jordan" because he seemed to fly! His dazzling skills helped the Chicago Bulls win six championships, making them the best team in the world. Michael's energy and enthusiasm for the game inspired kids to pick up a basketball and start shooting for the stars.

Michael Jordan's journey is a story of passion, persistence, and believing in oneself. Just like him, you have the power to turn your dreams into reality. Remember, even when things get tough, you can soar above challenges, just like Air Jordan soared above the basketball court. So, lace up your shoes, chase your dreams, and remember that you have the potential to be a superstar in your own life!

LESSONS FROM MICHAEL'S JOURNEY:

- **Believe in Yourself:** When things don't go as planned, remember that Michael Jordan didn't give up when he faced challenges. He believed in himself and kept going, turning his failures into stepping stones to success.

- **Work Hard:** Michael didn't become a legend overnight. He practiced and practiced, putting in the effort to get better every day. Hard work is the key to unlocking your potential.

- **Stay Determined:** There were times when Michael could've quit, but he didn't. He kept pushing forward with determination, and that's how he achieved greatness. You can do the same by not giving up on your dreams.

- **Help Others:** Being great isn't just about personal achievements; it's about making a positive impact on the world around you. Michael Jordan showed us that helping others is a wonderful way to share your success.

LEBRON JAMES

"Believe in yourself and all that you are. Know that there is something inside you that is greater than any obstacle." - **Lebron James**

Lebron James was born and raised in the vibrant city of Akron, Ohio. From a very early age, LeBron showed an incredible passion for the game. He would dribble a basketball around the neighborhood, imagining he was playing in front of thousands of cheering fans.

LeBron's family didn't have a lot of money, but they had an abundance of love and support. His mother, Gloria, had him when she was only 16 years old. She worked tirelessly to make ends meet, while his father was an ex-convict who spent more time in jail and wasn't present at all when he was growing up. LeBron's biggest dream was to one day play in the National Basketball Association (NBA). He knew it would be a long journey, but he believed in himself and his abilities.

At age 8, Lebron joined a pee wee football league where he met one of his teammates' father and pee wee football coach Frank Walker. At that time, his mom Gloria was moving so frequently and their living situation was becoming so uncertain. Lebron had to miss 82 out of 160 days of school that year! Coach Frank Walker and his wife Pam realized that Gloria was thinking about a new place for her son to live. They proposed that LeBron come live with them until Gloria could find stability again.

A year later, after some persuasion from Coach Frank Walker, LeBron joined his first rec-league basketball team, the Summit Lake Community Center Hornets. He then joined an AAU traveling youth league basketball team, the Shooting Stars, about a year later. He had a determination that shone brighter than any spotlight. He practiced every day after school, shooting baskets and perfecting his skills. His hard work and dedication caught the attention of his coaches, who saw the potential within him.

LeBron's talent on the court began to attract attention from high school scouts. He joined the varsity team at St. Vincent-St. Mary High School and quickly became a star player. He led his basketball team to three state titles and was named "Mr. Basketball" in Ohio for three straight years. But with fame came challenges. LeBron faced doubters who thought he was too young to make it big. He was also juggling his responsibilities as a student with his commitment to basketball.

During those challenging times, LeBron remembered the quote that had inspired him from the beginning. He believed in himself and his dreams, and he used the obstacles as stepping stones to success. With the support of his family, friends, and Coach Johnson, he continued to work hard and shine both on and off the court.

As LeBron's high school career came to an end, scouts from colleges all around the country were eager to recruit him. He decided not to go to college and went straight to the NBA. It was a risky move, but LeBron's confidence and determination knew no bounds. He was selected as the first overall pick by the Cleveland Cavaliers in the 2003 NBA draft.

LeBron's transition to the professional league wasn't without its challenges. He faced stronger opponents, experienced losses, and encountered setbacks. But he never forgot the lessons he had learned – to believe in himself, work hard, and stay focused on his dreams. He pushed himself to improve every day, and slowly but surely, he began to make a name for himself in the NBA.

Years went by, and LeBron's impact extended beyond the basketball court. He used his platform to inspire and uplift others. He started the LeBron James Family Foundation, which aimed to empower young people in his hometown and beyond. Through his foundation, he provided scholarships, built schools, and created opportunities for children who faced challenges similar to his own.

LeBron's dedication to his community and his sport didn't go unnoticed. He led the Cleveland Cavaliers to their first NBA championship in 2016, fulfilling a promise he had made to the city years before. His leadership, resilience, and ability to unite his team taught everyone the importance of perseverance and teamwork.

As time passed, LeBron continued to achieve remarkable milestones on and off the court. He joined different teams, won more championships, and became an inspiration to millions around the world. His journey from a young boy shooting hoops in Akron to a global icon reminded everyone that dreams could come true with hard work, determination, and unwavering self-belief.

LeBron James' story is a testament to the power of self-belief, hard work, and the willingness to overcome challenges. So, as you go through life, remember LeBron's journey and the lessons he taught us all — that with a dream in your heart and determination in your soul, you can achieve anything you set your mind to.

LESSONS FROM LEBRON'S JOURNEY:

- **Believe in Yourself:** No matter your circumstances, believe in your abilities and dreams. Trust that you have the power to overcome challenges and achieve greatness.

- **Work Hard:** Success doesn't come easy. Put in the effort, practice, and dedication needed to reach your goals.

- **Persevere Through Challenges:** Obstacles will come your way, but don't let them deter you. Use setbacks as opportunities to learn and grow stronger.

- **Teamwork and Leadership:** Just like LeBron's success relied on his team, remember that working together and supporting each other can lead to incredible achievements.

- **Give Back:** As you achieve your goals, remember to give back to your community and help those in need. Even small actions can make a big impact.

- **Stay Humble:** No matter how successful you become, humility and gratitude are important qualities to maintain.

LARRY BIRD

"Push yourself again and again. Don't give an inch until the final buzzer sounds." - **Larry Bird**

Larry Bird was born in West Baden Springs, Indiana, but raised in a nearby town called French Lick (Hence, the nickname *"The Hick from French Lick"*). Larry was not like the other kids in town. He was tall, lanky, and had a passion for basketball that burned brighter than the sun. He faced his fair share of struggles that tested his determination and resolve. Despite his burning passion for basketball, life wasn't always easy for young Larry.

Larry was born into a humble family that didn't have much money. His mother, Gloria, had to work two jobs to support Larry and his 5 siblings. His father, Joe, was a Korean war veteran. Larry's parents divorced when he was in high school which affected him so much that he abandoned his family. This provided him with the perfect opportunity to dedicate all his time to basketball. About a year later, his father Joe took his own life. The death of his father, along with their family's poverty struggles, has always taken an emotional toll on Larry. Despite these challenges, Larry's family challenges and the lessons he learned from their struggles played a crucial role in his journey to becoming a basketball icon.

Larry has always loved playing all kinds of sports when he was younger. When he got to high school, he decided to focus only on basketball. One day, he discovered that he could be really good at basketball. So, he started practicing a lot to get even better at it.

Every morning, Larry would wake up before the sun rose and head to the basketball court near his house. With a worn-out basketball in his hand, he would practice dribbling, shooting, and passing for hours on end. Despite the challenges and setbacks, Larry never gave up. He knew that success requires hard work and determination.

Larry joined the Springs Valley High School basketball team. His frequent practices paid off and his skills made him stand out. He emerged as the school all-time top scorer and star player!

One day, a college scout came to watch one of Larry's games. Larry's team was losing badly, but he didn't let that affect his performance. He played with all his heart, making incredible shots and passing the ball like a true leader. The scout was impressed not only by Larry's skills but also by his determination and passion for the game. Larry was offered a scholarship to play for the Indiana State University team under the top mentor Bobby Knight, and he eagerly accepted the opportunity.

After only a month at that university though, Larry dropped out because of the overwhelming population of students. He returned to the town he grew up in and spent a year at Northwood Institute engaging in multiple jobs. A year later, he enrolled at Indiana State University in a different location and there he spent the next 3 years playing college basketball. With him as the leader, the team got to be in the NCAA tournament for the first time. This tournament was a big deal and had a big impact on Larry's future in basketball. Even though his team didn't win the championship, Larry did amazing on the court and even got named the Player of the Year because of how well he played!

After college, Larry was drafted into the NBA by the Boston Celtics. He joined a team that had been struggling for a while, but Larry was determined to make a difference. He worked tirelessly, pushing himself and his teammates to be better every day. His incredible shooting accuracy and basketball IQ set him apart from other players.

Larry's rivalry with another legendary player, Magic Johnson, became the stuff of basketball history. Their intense battles on the court captivated fans all over the world. Larry's dedication to his craft and his never-back-down attitude inspired countless young athletes to pursue their dreams relentlessly.

But it wasn't just Larry's skills that made him a true basketball icon. He was known for his humility, sportsmanship, and love for the game. He never let fame get to his head, always acknowledging the efforts of his teammates and the support of his fans. Larry understood that it wasn't just about winning; it was about the journey, the effort, and the joy of playing the game he loved.

Years went by and Larry led the Celtics to three NBA championships. He won numerous awards and accolades, solidifying his place among the basketball greats. But even after all his achievements, Larry remained the same hardworking and humble boy from French Lick, Indiana.

As Larry's playing days came to an end, he continued to inspire others. He became a coach and an executive in the NBA, sharing his knowledge and passion with the next generation of players. Larry's story taught young athletes that success is not just about natural talent, but about dedication, perseverance, and a love for what you do.

Larry Bird's story is a testament to the power of determination, hard work, and a never-give-up attitude. He soared to unimaginable heights, not just as a basketball player, but as an inspiration to all those who dare to dream. Remember, just like Larry, you have the potential to make your dreams come true if you believe in yourself and put in the effort.

LESSONS FROM LARRY'S JOURNEY:

- **Dream Big:** Larry's story reminds us that dreams have no limits. No matter where you come from or how big your dreams are, with hard work and determination, you can achieve them.

- **Embrace Challenges:** Larry faced challenges and setbacks throughout his journey, but he never let them deter him. Instead, he used them as stepping stones to success.

- **Work Hard:** Larry's relentless practice and dedication to improving his skills set him apart. Hard work is the key to achieving your goals.

- **Believe in Yourself:** Even when others doubted him, Larry never doubted himself. Trusting in your abilities is crucial to achieving success.

- **Humility and Sportsmanship:** Larry's humility and sportsmanship on and off the court remind us that true greatness goes beyond talent. Treating others with respect and kindness is just as important.

- **Never Give Up:** Larry's journey was filled with ups and downs, but he never gave up on his dreams. Even when things got tough, he kept pushing forward.

- **Enjoy the Journey**: Winning is important, but enjoying the process and the love for what you do are equally valuable. Larry's passion for basketball always shone through, win or lose.

KOBE BRYANT

> "Everything negative -- pressure, challenges -- is all an opportunity for me to rise." - **Kobe Bryant**

Kobe Bryant is renowned for his status as one of the best basketball players in the history of the NBA. He dedicated twenty years of his career to the Los Angeles Lakers as a guard. He was known for his defensive skills, impressive vertical leap, and the knack for securing game-winning baskets during crucial moments. He is widely acknowledged as one of the best basketball players of the 2000s and perhaps one of the best of all time.

Kobe was born in Philadelphia, Pennsylvania to parents Joe "Jellybean" Bryant and Pamela Cox Bryant. Fun fact: He was named after the Japanese steak "kobe"! His dad Joe was a pro-basketball player so from a very young age, Kobe was determined to achieve greatness on the basketball court. He would spend hours practicing his shots, dribbling, and perfecting his moves.

When Kobe was six years old, he faced his first major challenge when his family moved to Italy so his dad could continue his basketball career overseas. Adjusting to a new country and culture was tough but Kobe embraced the opportunity to learn and grow. He spent a lot of his childhood there and played both basketball and soccer becoming huge fans of the Los Angeles Lakers as well as the A.C. Milan soccer team. He continued to improve his skills and make new friends. He also learned to speak fluent Italian! Kobe's dedication and hard work during these years would later become the foundation of his success.

On Sundays, when his dad Joe played for his new basketball team in Italy, Kobe would help out by mopping the sweat off the floors during breaks. After ensuring the court was spotless, he would grab a basketball and captivate the audience with his own spectacular performance. He would copy his dad's moves — dribbling between his legs, practicing his jumper, attempting to shoot from too far out — and the crowd just loved him! He would only leave the court when the officials insisted!

Even at a young age, Kobe already exhibited a very strong work ethic. He would hit the gym at 6 am when the rest of his junior team wouldn't show up until 9 am. He would also play through the pain — one time, he broke his dominant right hand but he managed to catch the ball with his weaker left and still made a three-pointer!

At thirteen years old, Kobe's dad moved their whole family back to Philadelphia. This was another major challenge for Kobe as he struggled to readjust to life and culture in the US. It was difficult as a teenager to engage with other kids his age as he didn't know the new slang they were using or any shared cultural references in TV or music. He was even made fun of for the clothes that he wore!

Kobe joined the basketball varsity team at Lower Merion High School. His talent and skills shone brightly during these high school years and he quickly became a star player. He won multiple special awards during his time there and even led the team to their first state championship in 53 years! He caught the attention of college scouts and even NBA teams. Despite scholarship offers from nearly every major college, Kobe decided not to attend college and went straight into professional basketball.

At the age of 17, Kobe achieved his dream of playing in the NBA. He was drafted initially by the Charlotte Hornets but got traded immediately to the Los Angeles Lakers, a team that would become his second family. Playing alongside experienced players, Kobe soaked up knowledge like a sponge. He studied their moves, learned from their experiences, and continued to refine his skills. His experience in Italy shaped Kobe for the better. *"By growing up in Italy,"* he reflected, *"I learned to play basketball the right way through a teaching of fundamentals first."* His work ethic inspired not only his teammates but basketball fans around the world. Kobe's commitment to hard work and his unwavering focus on improvement earned him the nickname "The Black Mamba." This wasn't just a nickname; it was a mindset—a relentless pursuit of excellence that he carried with him throughout his life.

Kobe's journey was not without obstacles. He faced tough opponents and heartbreaking losses, but he never let failure define him. Instead, he used setbacks as motivation to become even better. In 2000, Kobe and his Lakers team won their first NBA championship, the first of many. His hard work and determination had paid off, and he was an inspiration to everyone who watched him play.

As Kobe's basketball career flourished, he also explored his creativity off the court. He wrote books, created short films, and even won an Academy Award. Kobe's dedication to his craft showed that the Mamba Mentality could be applied to any field. He proved that with determination and a strong work ethic, you could achieve greatness no matter what you set your mind to.

Kobe Bryant's life was tragically cut short in a helicopter crash, but his legacy lives on. He will always be remembered as a shining example of what can be achieved through hard work, determination, and a never-give-up attitude. As long as there are stars in the sky and dreams in our hearts, the memory of Kobe Bryant will continue to inspire generations to come.

As you look up at the night sky, remember the story of Kobe Bryant. Just like him, you have the power to chase your dreams and make them a reality. It won't always be easy, but with the right mindset and a lot of hard work, you can achieve amazing things. So, shoot for the stars, embrace challenges, and always remember the lessons of the Mamba Mentality. Your journey is just beginning, and the world is waiting to see the incredible things you'll achieve.

LESSONS FROM KOBE'S JOURNEY:

- **Hard Work Pays Off**: Kobe's dedication to practicing and improving his skills led him to become one of the greatest basketball players of all time. No matter what your dream is, hard work is the key to success.

- **Embrace Challenges**: Moving to a new country was tough for Kobe, but he turned it into an opportunity to learn and grow. Don't be afraid of challenges; they can help you become stronger and more resilient.

- **Mamba Mentality**: The relentless pursuit of excellence, known as the Mamba Mentality, teaches us to give our best effort in everything we do. Whether it's sports, school, or hobbies, always strive for your personal best.

- **Learn from Failure**: Kobe faced setbacks and losses, but he used them as motivation to improve. Don't let failure discourage you—use it as a stepping stone to success.

- **Inspire Others:** Kobe inspired teammates, fans, and people around the world with his passion and work ethic. You too can inspire others by being dedicated, kind, and always doing your best.

KEVIN DURANT

"I've learned what it feels like to lose, believe me. But I think in the end, that is just going to make winning that much better." - **Kevin Durant**

Kevin Durant stands tall as one of the NBA's most remarkable athletes leaving a lasting mark on the league. Presently donning the jersey of the Brooklyn Nets, this two-time NBA Finals MVP also made waves as a vital member of the Golden State Warriors. However, Kevin's path to success was far from smooth. His childhood is a narrative of challenges, and he often shares his journey in interviews shedding light on the hardships he encountered while growing up.

Kevin was born in Washington DC to parents Wanda Durant and Wayne Pratt. Kevin was only 9 months old when his father Wayne decided to leave their family which led to a divorce between his parents. His mother Wanda didn't have the money to rent an apartment, so she decided to live with her mother, Kevin's grandmother, who helped raise Kevin and his brother while Wanda worked long hours to make ends meet. All these unfortunate circumstances caused Kevin to experience a lot of turmoil at such a young age. Frequently, Kevin found himself having to look after his own needs, and he has shared that he experienced hunger on numerous occasions during his childhood.

Kevin never fails to speak about the sacrifices that his mother made during his formative years. When Kevin was just 10 years old, he made a choice to become a basketball player. His mother pledged her support, consistently urging him throughout his career to put in the work and maintain his physical condition. Kevin acknowledges a significant portion of his accomplishments to his mother's influence and guidance. When Kevin turned 13, his father Wayne came back into his life. He has apologized multiple times and regretted leaving his family. Wayne has been inseparable with Kevin since he came back into his life.

Despite these hardships, Kevin was able to find success on the basketball court. As he grew older, Kevin's skills blossomed. He joined his school's basketball team and showcased his extraordinary talent. He was a standout player in high school. Kevin's passion for the game and his willingness to learn were evident in every practice and game. Kevin continued to put in the work, and he eventually earned a scholarship to play at the University of Texas where he dazzled everyone with his incredible skills. His ability to score from anywhere on the court was simply magical. Kevin's college coach often said, "He's not just a great player; he's an inspiration to all his teammates." Kevin's freshman year at Texas was truly remarkable. He won numerous Player of the Year awards, including the esteemed Naismith and Wooden awards. This achievement was particularly impressive for a freshman and showcased his readiness to ascend into a superstar at a higher level.

Kevin's journey wasn't without its challenges. He faced doubts and setbacks, including injuries that tested his resolve. But he refused to give up. With each obstacle, he worked harder, rehabilitated diligently, and came back stronger. His determination was unbreakable.

Finally, the day came when Kevin's dream turned into reality. He was selected as the second overall pick in the 2007 NBA Draft by the Seattle SuperSonics. From that moment on, he was known as Kevin Durant, an NBA player with a heart full of determination and a spirit that refused to quit.

Throughout his NBA career, Kevin's dedication and hard work continued to shine. He played for several teams, including the Oklahoma City Thunder and the Golden State Warriors. His incredible scoring ability and versatility made him a force to be reckoned with on the court. Fans from around the world admired his skills, but they also admired his humility and sportsmanship. Kevin's story is one of resilience and triumph. He faced adversity with a smile, turned setbacks into comebacks, and always believed in his abilities.

Kevin's childhood struggles taught him the value of hard work, determination, and perseverance. He learned that success doesn't come easy and that overcoming obstacles is a crucial part of any journey. These challenges not only fueled his passion for basketball but also instilled in him the importance of resilience, empathy, and giving back to his community. Kevin's journey from a young boy living in poverty, shooting hoops at the park because he fell in love with the game, to an NBA superstar is an inspiration to all. He reminds us that with passion, perseverance, and belief in ourselves, we can rise above any challenge and reach great heights. So, dream big like Kevin, and let your determination light the path to your own success.

LESSONS FROM KEVIN'S JOURNEY:

- **Financial Hardships:** Kevin's family didn't have a lot of money, which meant that he often had to make do with less. He didn't always have the latest sneakers or basketball gear like some of his peers. Despite this, his love for the game was unwavering. He would play basketball in hand-me-down shoes and sometimes even play barefoot, showing his dedication to the sport.

- **Limited Resources:** The neighborhood where Kevin lived didn't have the best basketball facilities. The courts were sometimes run-down and not well-maintained. This meant that he had to practice on less-than-ideal surfaces. Despite the lack of proper facilities, Kevin made the best of what he had, using his local park's court to hone his skills.

- **Peer Pressure and Negative Influences:** Growing up in a tough neighborhood, Kevin was surrounded by peer pressure and negative influences. Some of his friends got involved in activities that could have led him down the wrong path. However, Kevin's passion for basketball kept him focused and gave him a positive outlet to channel his energy. He chose the basketball court over the streets, a decision that ultimately shaped his future.

- **Family Support:** In spite of the hardships during Kevin's childhood, he did have a strong support system in his family, he also faced the challenge of wanting to make his loved ones proud. He knew that his family believed in him and his dreams, and he didn't want to let them down. This pressure could have been overwhelming, but Kevin turned it into motivation to work harder and achieve his goals.

- **Embrace Hard Work:** Success doesn't come overnight. Hard work and dedication are the keys to achieving your goals. Even when things get tough, keep pushing forward.

- **Believe in Yourself:** No matter where you start, believe in your dreams and your abilities. Have confidence in yourself, and you'll be surprised by what you can achieve.

JIMMY BUTLER

"It's not all fine and dandy, but a smile can go a long way. Show some love, be patient, and this world will be a much better place." **- Jimmy Butler**

In the world of basketball, if there's one player who truly embodies the spirit of determination and hard work, that would be Jimmy Butler. From a challenging childhood to becoming a superstar in the NBA, Jimmy's journey is a story of perseverance, passion, and the belief that anything is possible.

Jimmy was born in the outskirts of Houston, Texas, in a small town called Tomball. His father left his mom when he was just a baby and so he was raised by a single parent during his early years. When Jimmy was 13 years old, his mother kicked him out of the house saying *"I don't like the look of you. You gotta go."*

Jimmy basically became homeless overnight and was forced to bounce from one friend's home to another. He did this for the majority of his teenage years until his senior year when he met Jordan Leslie. Jordan also played football and basketball at Tomball High School, they hit it off and became very good friends. Jimmy started staying at Jordan's house and after a few months of him staying over, Jordan's very loving mother, Michelle Lambert, welcomed Jimmy with open arms and made him a part of their already big family. They took him in in spite of them already having 7 kids at their house! This family bond provided Butler with the support he required during that phase of his life, allowing him to dedicate himself entirely to the game of basketball.

In high school, he joined his school's basketball team and worked tirelessly to improve his skills. He excelled at the game and was voted by his teammates as the most valuable player. In spite of his excellent skills on the court, Jimmy wasn't heavily recruited coming out of high school. He opted to attend Tyler Junior College where he continued to work hard and practice to really hone his skills.

His hard work paid off when he received an athletic scholarship to play basketball at Marquette University. College wasn't just about basketball for Jimmy; it was a chance to prove that he could excel both on and off the court.

In 2011, Jimmy's dreams took a giant leap forward when he was selected in the first round of the NBA Draft by the Chicago Bulls. This was a dream come true, but Jimmy knew that the real work was just beginning. He continued to push himself to be the best player he could be. He was known for his incredible work ethic — arriving at the gym early, staying late, and giving his all in every practice and game.

As Jimmy's skills improved, so did his reputation in the NBA. He became known for his relentless defense, his ability to score in clutch moments, and his leadership on and off the court. He played with teams like the Chicago Bulls, Minnesota Timberwolves, Philadelphia

76ers, and finally, the Miami Heat. With each team, he left a mark of hard work and dedication.

Today, Jimmy Butler is not only a basketball star but also a symbol of hope and inspiration. His journey from a tough childhood to NBA stardom shows that with determination, hard work, and a belief in oneself, anyone can overcome challenges and reach for the stars. So, if you ever feel like giving up or think that your dreams are too big, remember Jimmy Butler's story – a story of rising from hardship to basketball stardom, and let it inspire you to chase your own dreams with unwavering determination.

LESSONS FROM JIMMY'S JOURNEY:

- **Believe in Yourself:** No matter where you come from or what challenges you face, believe in your own potential. Jimmy never let his tough upbringing stop him from dreaming big and believing in his abilities.

- **Work Hard:** Success doesn't come easy. Jimmy's story teaches us that hard work and dedication are essential to achieving your goals. He put in countless hours of practice to become the player he is today.

- **Persevere Through Challenges**: Life will throw obstacles your way, but don't give up. Jimmy faced difficulties but used them as stepping stones to move forward. Remember, challenges are opportunities in disguise.

- **Stay Humble:** Despite his fame and success, Jimmy remained humble and grounded. He never forgot where he came from and used his platform to inspire others.

- **Teamwork and Leadership:** Basketball, like life, is about teamwork and leadership. Jimmy's ability to lead his teammates and work together towards a common goal is a valuable lesson for all of us.

CARON BUTLER

> "He who expects not to achieve will never do so."
> **- Caron Butler**

Imagine growing up in a neighborhood where challenges seemed to be around every corner. Imagine facing obstacles that might have held others back, but you found a way to rise above them. This is the inspiring story of Caron Butler, a true champion both on and off the basketball court.

From a young age, Caron faced difficulties that would have discouraged many. His neighborhood was often plagued by crime and poverty. In his early years in Racine, Wisconsin, Caron never even entertained the idea of making it to the NBA. Instead, his focus was directed towards the constant challenge of finding his next source of income.

Caron's mother frequently worked multiple jobs to provide for him and his brother. Seeing his mom work so much and so hard to support them pushed Caron to a life of crime.

At the young age of 12, Caron was already selling drugs on the streets and by the time he reached 15 years old, he had already encountered the law on 15 separate occasions. A moment that truly shaped his life was witnessing his mother in tears behind the windows of a police car. This experience became the turning point that motivated him to completely transform his life for the better. Inspired by his mother's pain, Butler unearthed his deep love for basketball during his time at a youth detention center where he was sentenced for 18 months. It was there that he channeled his energy and determination into training and turning his life around.

After he was released from prison, Caron enrolled in school, got a job at a nearby Burger King, and really made sincere efforts to steer clear of any further entanglements with the law. Basketball became Caron's escape from the struggles of his everyday life. He found solace on the court, where his determination and talent shone brightly. Caron's dedication to the sport was unmatched. He spent countless hours practicing, even in less-than-ideal conditions.

Caron played basketball in the Amateur Athletic Union between 1998 and 1999. He had a brief career at Racine Park High School and then enrolled at Marine Central Institute. Throughout his time at the institution, Butler honed his basketball skills, refining his game to a higher level. This dedication paid off as he earned a valuable scholarship opportunity to join the ranks of Coach Jim Calhoun's team at the renowned Big East powerhouse, the University of Connecticut. This was a turning point in his life. He was determined to make the most of this opportunity and worked tirelessly to improve his game. Caron's perseverance led him to become a standout player, catching the attention of professional scouts.

Caron's journey took him to the NBA when he was selected as the 10th overall pick in the 2002 draft by the Miami Heat. He proved himself to be a force to be reckoned with on the court, earning the nickname "Tuff Juice" for his tough playing style. Caron's dedication, combined with his incredible work ethic, led him to have a successful career in the NBA, playing for several teams including the Washington Wizards and the Los Angeles Lakers. He retired in 2018 and is now the assistant coach of the Miami Heat.

Caron Butler's story is a true testament to the power of determination, hard work, and a positive attitude. He turned a challenging upbringing into a source of strength, using his experiences to motivate and inspire others. Caron's journey reminds us that no matter where we come from, we have the power to shape our own destinies and achieve greatness.

So, the next time you face a difficult situation or think that your dreams are too big, remember Caron Butler's story. Remember that with perseverance, hard work, and a belief in yourself, you can rise above any challenge and make your dreams a reality.

LESSONS FROM CARON'S JOURNEY:

- **Perseverance Pays Off:** Caron's life was full of challenges, but he never gave up. He turned setbacks into comebacks through sheer determination and hard work. No matter how tough things got, he kept pushing forward.

- **Dream Big:** Caron's story teaches us that no dream is too big, even if it seems impossible. He dared to dream of a better life and worked relentlessly to make it happen.

- **Resilience in the Face of Adversity:** Life is full of obstacles, but Caron showed us that we can overcome anything if we believe in ourselves and stay resilient.

- **Learning from Mistakes:** Caron made mistakes, but he didn't let them define him. He used them as stepping stones to a better future.

- **Giving Back:** Caron's success didn't just benefit him. He used his platform to give back to his community and inspire others to rise above their challenges.

DWYANE WADE

"My belief is stronger than your doubt."
– Dwyane Wade

In the heart of Chicago, Illinois lived a young boy named Dwyane Wade. His life was a journey of challenges and triumphs, teaching him that with determination and courage, one could overcome any obstacle. This is the inspiring story of Dwyane Wade's childhood, a story that proves how even in the face of adversity, dreams can come true.

Dwyane was only 4 months old when his parents separated. His mother, JoLinda, got custody of him and his older sister Tragil. Sadly, JoLinda got addicted to drugs and frequently engaged in unlawful activities leading to her being put to jail. When Dwyane was just eight years old, his sister Tragil played a trick on him. She led him to believe they were just going to the movies, but instead, she took him to a different neighborhood where his father lived with his new wife. Tragil actually brought Dwyane to live with his father and stepmother which turned out to be such a great blessing! This move changed the course of Dwyane's life, guiding him away from the crime-infested environment of his early days.

Dwyane continued to visit his mother in jail but a year later, his father relocated the family to Robbins, Illinois which is a suburb in the southern part of Chicago. Dwyane wasn't able to see his mother for the next 2 years because of this move.

In his new surroundings, Dwyane had the opportunity to engage in basketball games outdoors. He joined his step brothers, newfound friends, and his father, who actually served as a part-time coach at a local recreation center.

Dwyane eventually enrolled at Harold L. Richards High School in Oak Lawn, where his older stepbrother Demetrius had already established his reputation as the basketball team's standout player. He played both basketball and football and actually excelled more at football playing as a wide receiver and occasionally, back up quarterback. He never lost his love for basketball. He worked very hard to secure a spot on the varsity basketball team's regular lineup during his junior year. Through dedicated practice, he honed his ball-handling techniques and sharpened his outside game. It also helped a lot that he experienced a growth spurt of almost four inches, propelling his height to over 6 feet. As a result of his efforts, Wade rose as the shining star of the basketball team!

His success in basketball continued all throughout senior year but that doesn't mean everything came easy to Dwyane now. He faced more obstacles in high school. His grades sometimes slipped, causing him to be suspended from the basketball team. It was a tough wake-up call, but Dwyane was not one to stay down for long. He used this setback to fuel his determination, turning his focus to academics and ensuring that his dreams were never compromised again.

Getting a college scholarship wasn't easy, especially with Dwyane's low grades, and he was only recruited by 3 basketball programs. He chose to accept the scholarship program from Marquette University in Milwaukee, Wisconsin. His low grades made him ineligible to play but his head coach Tom Crean took him in as a partial qualifier. This arrangement allowed Wade to still be part of the team, although he had to sit out from playing during the 2000-01 season. He was also still allowed to continue to attend school and train with the team. During this time, he diligently worked on refining his skills and tutoring helped him with his academics. When sophomore year came, Dwyane emerged with even greater prowess!

In his junior year, Dwyane's success continued. He led Marquette to their school's first Conference USA Championship as well as the NCAA! He continued to be the lead scorer and was even chosen as the MVP of the MIdwest Regional Finals! Dwyane decided to skip senior year and went straight to entering the 2003 NBA draft. He was selected by the Miami Heat with the fifth overall pick.

Dwyane's first year with the Miami Heat was incredible! He was performing very well with averages of 16.2 points, 4.5 assists, and 4.0 rebounds per game. This earned him a unanimous selection to the 2004 NBA All-Rookie team! He also got to play alongside one of his idols, Shaquille O'Neal, which made him perform even better and his average numbers increased even further!

Dwyane's legacy extends far beyond the basketball court. He used his fame to make a difference in the world. He became an advocate for equality, justice, and helping those in need. He started initiatives to support children and uplift communities. Dwyane showed that being a hero was about more than just winning games; it was about using your influence to inspire change.

Dwyane Wade's journey from a challenging childhood to becoming a basketball legend and a force for good is a story of courage, resilience, and hope. It reminds us that no matter where we start, our dreams are within reach if we work hard and never give up. Just like Dwyane, you have the power to rise above all odds and make your dreams come true.

LESSONS FROM DWYANE'S JOURNEY:

- **Believe in Yourself:** No matter your size or background, believing in yourself can lead to greatness. Always believe that you are meant for more! Dwyane believing in himself and his abilities allowed him to rise above the doubts and become one of the greatest basketball players in the world.

- **Persevere Through Challenges:** Challenges are like stepping stones; with each one, you grow stronger. Never give up at the first sign of failure. Dwyane faced family struggles and academic setbacks but he never gave up. He saw each challenge as an opportunity to learn and become stronger. Just like stepping stones in a river, each obstacle he overcame made him more resilient. When he couldn't play due to academic issues in college, he didn't quit. Instead, he used that time to work on his skills and come back even better. Challenges weren't roadblocks for him; they were chances to grow.

- **Family and Support:** Surround yourself with people who uplift and believe in you. His sister, Tragil, might have played a trick on him, but deep down, she wanted what was best for him. When he moved in with his father and stepmother, he found a supportive environment that helped him flourish. The people who loved and believed in Dwyane became his strength. They reminded him that he wasn't alone in his journey. Surrounding yourself with people who uplift and believe in you can be a powerful source of motivation.

- **Make a Difference:** Success is sweeter when you use it to make the world a better place. Dwyane Wade's success didn't stop at becoming a famous basketball player. He used his fame and influence to make a positive impact on the world. He stood up for equality and justice, advocating for important causes. He started initiatives to help children in need and supported communities facing challenges. Dwyane understood that success wasn't just about personal achievements; it was about how you can make a difference in the lives of others. He showed that using your success to make the world better brings a deeper sense of fulfillment.

JEREMY LIN

All these people, all these things came into my life, and they're all blessings from God. And now that I look back, I realize that these are His fingerprints all over my story. - **Jeremy Lin**

Many of the stories we've explored in this book have featured athletes who faced tough beginnings due to financial hardships. Jeremy Lin's journey was unique, characterized by challenges stemming from racial stereotypes. Let's explore Jeremy's early years pre-NBA as he showcases why you should never give up on your dream.

Jeremy was born in Torrance, CA to Taiwanese immigrant parents Gie-ming Lin and Shirley Lin. From an early age, he loved dribbling and shooting hoops, dreaming of becoming a professional basketball player one day. His parents were very supportive and enrolled him in a local YMCA to learn and practice basketball. They have always encouraged him to follow his dreams, reminding him that hard work and determination were key to achieving anything he set his mind to.

Jeremy became a star player at Palo Alto High School, earning the role of team captain in his senior year — that same year, his team secured the state championship. He also won individual awards, including regional Player of the Year. Alongside his athletic abilities, Jeremy also displayed exceptional academic performance, achieving top grades across all his subjects. He also took on the role of editor for his high school newspaper and even undertook a summer internship with California Senator Joe Simitian. Jeremy was not just a star athlete but a star student as well!

With high grades and exceptional basketball skills, you would think college scouts will be knocking down his door, right? Jeremy didn't get a single scholarship offer. Jeremy had to send his résumé along with a DVD showcasing highlights from his high school basketball journey to the top Ivy League institutions: the University of California, Berkeley, Stanford University, UCLA, to name a few. Among these options, Harvard and Brown were the only ones who assured him a place on their teams; however, Ivy League schools don't provide athletic scholarships. He opted to enroll in Harvard but where they let him play for their basketball team as a walk-on, meaning he wasn't guaranteed a spot on the team. Jeremy faced tough competition, but his work ethic and determination caught the coach's attention, and he earned his place on the team.

Harvard's assistant coach, Bill Holden, held reservations about Lin's basketball skills initially describing him as a "Division III player". However, his perception changed after he saw Jeremy's performance in a more intense game where he fearlessly drove to the basket at every chance. Subsequently, Jeremy became a force to be reckoned with and emerged as Harvard's most sought-after recruit.

Jeremy's college career wasn't without its struggles. He faced doubts from those who thought Ivy League players couldn't compete with athletes from bigger schools. Being one of the few, or the only, Asian-American player in his league, Jeremy faced challenges on the court that weren't always simple to navigate. He would have racial slurs from both spectators and opponents hurled at him, yet he refused to allow these hurtful remarks to discourage him. Jeremy's performance spoke for itself. He consistently improved and proved his doubters wrong. His senior year was particularly impressive, and he led his team to a successful season.

Despite his college success, Jeremy faced yet another hurdle: getting into the NBA. He went undrafted which was very disappointing but again, he didn't let that deter him. Jeremy attended the mini-camp for the Dallas Mavericks as well as the NBA Summer League team. After 5 games at the Summer League, he finally got invitations from the Mavericks, Los Angeles Lakers, and the Golden State Warriors! He signed with the Golden State Warriors as a free agent and they even held a press conference for him, which was something they've never done for an undrafted rookie! But Jeremy was special – the large Asian-American community in the San Francisco Bay Area has been following his progress and they all showed up to support the first ever Asian-American of Taiwanese descent to ever step foot in the NBA!

With the Warriors, Jeremy's playing time was limited. He was even sent down to the NBA Development League at times. But Jeremy kept working hard and never lost sight of his dream. While Jeremy earned praise for his unwavering dedication and remarkable progress, he faced a setback when he was released by the Golden State team at the start of the 2011–12 season. Swiftly, he was picked up and subsequently released by the Houston Rockets. However, Jeremy's fortunes changed when he joined the New York Knicks in late December 2011.

In February 2012, while playing for the New York Knicks, Jeremy got his chance to shine. With several key players injured, he was given the opportunity to play significant minutes. Jeremy took full advantage of it. He had an astonishing run of games where he played at an incredibly high level, leading to a phenomenon known as "Linsanity." Jeremy's story captured the hearts of fans around the world, showing that hard work and perseverance could lead to incredible success. He quickly became an instrumental part of a seven-game winning streak, even earning more points than the legendary Kobe Bryant in a match-up against the Los Angeles Lakers.

Jeremy's impact extended beyond the basketball court. He used his platform to advocate for important issues, including equality and inclusion. He also started the Jeremy Lin Foundation, which focuses on empowering underprivileged children and communities through education, leadership development, and promoting healthy living.

As Jeremy Lin's basketball career continued, he inspired countless people with his story. He showed that with passion, hard work, and a positive attitude, we can overcome any challenge and achieve our dreams. His journey reminds us that success is not just about winning games, but about the person we become along the way.

LESSONS FROM JEREMY'S JOURNEY:

- **Believe in Yourself:** Despite doubts and setbacks, Jeremy never stopped believing in his abilities. He teaches us to have confidence in ourselves, even when others doubt us.

- **Embrace Challenges:** Jeremy's journey was filled with challenges, but he used them as opportunities to grow and improve. He shows us that challenges can make us stronger.

- **Persevere:** Even when things got tough, Jeremy never gave up. His rise to fame didn't come easy and Jeremy had to earn every opportunity he could get because they were few and far between. His determination to overcome obstacles reminds us to keep pushing forward, no matter what.

- **Make a Positive Impact:** Jeremy used his success to make a positive impact on the world. He teaches us the importance of giving back and using our influence for good.

ALLEN IVERSON

I failed, got back up. I failed, got back up.
- **Allen Iverson**

Allen Ezail Iverson was born on June 7, 1975, in Hampton, Virginia. He had a very rough childhood and was raised by a single mom after his father deserted them when he was just an infant. His mom later moved to an apartment with her boyfriend, Michael Freeman, who became Allen's father figure.

When Allen was about 13 years old, Michael got arrested right in front of him for dealing drugs. Life after that got worse for Allen and his sister as their living conditions became extremely poor and inhabitable. They moved around a lot and one of the places they lived in was so bad that they had to walk through knee-deep sewage!

From a young age, Allen has always been very athletic. He attended Bethel High School and participated, and excelled, in two very competitive sports, football and basketball! Allen took on the role of quarterback for the school's football team, simultaneously participating as a running back, kick returner, and defensive back. At the same time, he secured the position of point guard for the school's basketball team. In his junior year, Allen showcased exceptional leadership by guiding both teams to Virginia State Championships. His remarkable achievements extended to being honored with The Associated Press High School Player of the Year award in both football and basketball.

His success on the court, however, was often overshadowed by his troubled personal life. In 1993, he was involved in a brawl at a bowling alley. While there were different versions of the events — with Allen asserting that he left before the fight began — he was found guilty and was given a 15 year sentence to a correctional facility. He ended up staying there for only 4 months because the governor granted him a partial release as long as he can meet certain conditions.

While in the correctional facility, Allen still tried to stay strong. He said *"I had to use the whole jail situation as something positive. Going to jail, someone sees something weak in you, they'll exploit it. I never showed any weakness. I just kept going strong until I came out."*. Allen ended up finishing at a different high school for at-risk students when he came out of jail but his basketball performance at Bethel prior to jail was enough to prove to Georgetown University Coach John Thompson to come out and meet Allen and offer him a full scholarship!

Allen delivered outstanding performances at Georgetown. He would score an average of 22.9 points per game and even got the conference's Defensive Player of the Year award twice. During his second year, he guided their team to the NCAA Tournament's Elite 8 and earned the prestigious title of First-Team All American.

Allen didn't finish college after his sophomore year and decided to try for the NBA drafts. Allen's dream came true when he was selected as the first overall pick in the NBA Draft by the Philadelphia 76ers. He was actually the shortest 1st draft pick ever!

At the start of his NBA career, Allen was breaking records left and right! He scored above 30 points per game, some even going up to 40 and 50 points. His lightning-fast crossovers, fearless drives to the basket, and scoring ability made him a force to be reckoned with. Despite facing taller opponents, Allen's determination and passion allowed him to shine as one of the league's top players. He even did a very memorable cross-over with Michael Jordan, one of his idols! Allen was on fire at every game and was named the NBA Rookie of the Year.

While enjoying success in the NBA, Allen continued to face personal and professional challenges. He dealt with injuries that sidelined him for periods but he always fought his way back to the court. Off the court, because of his rebellious attitude, media scrutiny and negative attention was always around him but he remained resilient.

As Allen's career progressed, some people loved him and some people hated him. To those that did love him, he became an inspiration to many young basketball players who looked up to him. He showed them that hard work, determination, and a strong belief in oneself can lead to success, regardless of the obstacles one faces. He also emphasized the importance of staying true to one's unique style and identity.

Allen's journey teaches us valuable lessons. Despite facing challenges, he never gave up on his dreams. He showed us that setbacks can be stepping stones to success and that staying true to oneself is more important than conforming to others' expectations. His story reminds us that with passion, perseverance, and the right attitude, anyone can rise above their circumstances and achieve greatness.

Allen Iverson's life is a testament to the power of determination and self-belief. From his humble beginnings to his iconic moments on the basketball court, his journey is a source of inspiration for everyone, especially young readers facing their own challenges. Remember, just like Allen, you have the potential to rise above the odds and achieve your dreams, no matter how big they may be.

LESSONS FROM ALLEN'S JOURNEY:

- **Dream Big, Work Hard:** Despite his small stature and difficult circumstances, Iverson never stopped dreaming of becoming a professional basketball player. He showed that with hard work and dedication, even the loftiest dreams can become reality.

- **Resilience in the Face of Adversity**: Iverson faced numerous obstacles throughout his life, including personal struggles, legal troubles, and injuries. Yet, he always found a way to bounce back. His ability to overcome setbacks teaches us the importance of resilience and perseverance.

- **Stay True to Your Identity:** Iverson never tried to be someone he wasn't. He stayed true to his personality, style, and values, even when facing pressure to conform. This authenticity resonated with fans and showed that being genuine is more important than fitting in.

- **Turn Mistakes into Lessons:** Iverson openly acknowledged his mistakes and took responsibility for them. This demonstrates the importance of learning from our errors and using them as opportunities to grow and make positive changes.

DERRICK ROSE

As long as I have my faith in God, I'm good. I know everything else is going to come. - **Derrick Rose**

If there's one thing that Derrick Rose has that a lot of the other players in this book didn't, it's a tight-knit family who supported and disciplined him to be the best he can be in spite of their struggles. When they struggled, they struggled together – and when they thrived, they did it together too. Let us explore Derrick's rise to stardom together starting from his humble beginnings.

Derrick was born and raised in a little town called Englewood, in Chicago, Illinois. Englewood is known to be the most dangerous neighborhood on Chicago's south side. There, Derrick discovered his passion for the sport at an early age, dribbling a basketball around the cracked sidewalks in his neighborhood.

Growing up in a tough neighborhood, Derrick's very tight-knit family never gave him the chance to turn out like the rest of the kids who became drug dealers. Derrick's mother, Brenda, was very strict but also very loving. She wouldn't allow her children to become gangsters and would drag them back home when she heard that one of them was getting into trouble.

Derrick is the youngest of 4 boys and his older brothers – Dwayne, Reggie, and Allan – took on a fatherly role when it came to their baby brother. All 3 of his brothers were also very talented basketball players already. They taught Derrick everything he needed to know about the game. They were always by Derrick's side whether in school or in basketball practices. They also disciplined him when necessary.

By the eighth grade, Derrick's basketball skills were already apparent and he started to garner fame and attention in Chicago. His family were worried that street agents might manipulate his journey to the NBA, veering it off course, so they restricted outside contact to him. His brothers were always by Derrick's side whether in school or in basketball practices. They also disciplined him when necessary.

In 2003, Derrick started attending Simeon Academy in Chicago, and he quickly became one of the best high school players in the country. He had a very successful basketball career at the school and won many games and awards. When he was in his last year, he was considered the best high school point guard in the whole country! He scored an average of 25.2 points per game and led Simeon to win its second state title in a row with a record of 33 wins and only 2 losses. In that same year, he was even featured in the Chicago Tribune newspaper where they gave him the title of "Illinois Mr. Basketball" for 2007.

Not surprisingly, Derrick received many college basketball scholarship offers. He accepted the offer at the University of Memphis Tigers. He picked them because of the school's history of putting players in the NBA. He was also looking forward to having Rod

Strickland, a 17-year veteran of the league, mentoring him.

Derrick played his heart out at Memphis and he showcased not just his talents but also his determination and resilience by leading the Tigers to 38 total wins, which is the most wins in NCAA history!

In 2008, Derrick declared for the NBA Draft, and his dreams were about to become reality. He was selected as the first overall pick by the Chicago Bulls. While his journey to the NBA was a remarkable achievement, Derrick faced the pressure of high expectations and the physical demands of professional basketball. He encountered injuries that tested his resolve, but he refused to let them define him.

He also got involved in a controversy when the NCAA wrote a letter to Memphis in 2009 saying that Derrick's test score from the year before at Simeon High School in Chicago was not valid. Then, in the following January, the NCAA sent another letter accusing Memphis of being aware that Rose had someone else take his SAT test for him. Memphis began its own investigation and replied on April 24th. Reports also came out saying that Rose's brother, Reggie, had been given permission to travel with the team without having to pay on multiple occasions. Numerous back and forth investigations were exchanged but ultimately, Memphis couldn't find any proof that Rose had cheated and they cleared his name.

Derrick's perseverance paid off in the 2010-2011 NBA season when he led the Chicago Bulls to one of the best records in the league. His incredible performance earned him the title of NBA Most Valuable Player (MVP), making him the youngest player to ever receive this honor. This achievement showed young readers that hard work and determination can lead to extraordinary success.

While at the peak of his career, Derrick faced a series of heartbreaking injuries that threatened to end his basketball journey. He tore his ACL, underwent surgeries, and endured a long road to recovery. These setbacks were tough, but they didn't break Derrick's spirit. He used his challenges as fuel to come back even stronger, showing young readers that setbacks are a part of life, but they can be overcome with determination.

Derrick's story is a shining example of resilience, determination, and the power of dreams. Despite all the challenges he faced, he continued to rise above adversity and inspire those around him. His story teaches us that with hard work, passion, and an unbreakable spirit, anything is possible.

Derrick Rose's story continues to inspire generations, showing us that no challenge is too great to overcome. His journey from the tough streets of Chicago to NBA stardom is a testament to the power of perseverance and the belief that dreams can become a reality. As young readers, remember Derrick's story when faced with challenges – rise above, stay dedicated, and let your dreams soar.

LESSONS FROM DERRICK'S JOURNEY:

- **Believe in Yourself:** No matter where you come from or what challenges you face, believe in your abilities and dreams. Derrick's journey started from the streets of Chicago, and his unwavering belief in himself helped him achieve greatness.

- **Never Give Up:** Life is full of obstacles, but giving up should never be an option. Derrick's story teaches us that setbacks are just stepping stones towards success.

- **Work Hard and Stay Dedicated:** Success doesn't come easy. Derrick's countless hours of practice and dedication to improvement demonstrate that hard work is the key to achieving your goals.

- **Turn Challenges into Strengths:** Derrick's injuries could have ended his career, but he used them to become mentally and physically stronger. We can all learn from his ability to turn adversity into an advantage.

- **Inspire Others:** Derrick's journey has inspired countless people around the world. By staying true to yourself and pursuing your dreams, you can inspire those around you to do

GIANNIS ANTETOKOUNMPO

> Persistent in life? I think, yes, I am. I'm going to do something until I get it right.
> **- Giannis Antetokounmpo**

A lot of athletes in this book had a hard time growing up and Giannis is one with an even tougher start. His story is one of courage, perseverance, and the remarkable journey from a tough beginning to becoming a shining star.

Giannis' parents moved from Nigeria to Sepolia, a working-class neighborhood in Athens, Greece in search of a better life. This was where Giannis, as well as his 3 brothers, were born. Giannis's father was a soccer player in Nigeria and his mother was a high jumper. It seemed like athleticism already ran in the family but at this time, sports was probably the last thing on this family's minds.

Giannis' parents had dreams of a different future but fate had other plans. Life in Sepolia wasn't easy for the Antetokounmpo family and opportunities were scarce especially for undocumented migrants like them. They didn't have work permits and so both of Giannis' parents struggled to find work. Giannis' father worked as a handyman while his mother was a babysitter. Giannis and his brothers would occasionally help their parents earn some money by selling items on the streets like sunglasses and watches. Giannis became a determined salesman, never giving up until he made a sale. His secret weapon? Persistence and a touch of youthful charm.

Greece didn't offer birthright citizenship and as the children of Nigerian immigrants, they were never officially recognised as Greek citizens, and were considered "stateless". For the first 18 years of his life, Giannis and his family could not travel outside the country because they had no papers from Greece or Nigeria. There was also that constant fear of being kicked out of the country.

Another challenge the Antetokounmpo family faced was racism and discrimination. They never felt like they truly belonged. Growing up, Giannis sometimes felt as an outsider to both the Greek and the Nigerian communities in Athens because of their different skin color but also his inability to speak the Nigerian language.

Giannis's childhood wasn't easy. His family had to go through having to move all the time because they couldn't pay their rent anymore. He often went to bed hungry or went to school with no breakfast. He shared a bed with his brothers, lived with the constant fear of losing their home, and shouldered stresses beyond his years. Little did he know these very challenges were molding him into a person of great strength.

Even though their situation was tough, Giannis and his brothers found joy in sports. At first, they loved playing football, a popular game in Greece.

But everything shifted in 2007. A coach named Spiros Velliniatis noticed that 13-year-old Giannis had a lot of energy and strength. He talked to Giannis' mom and convinced her that basketball could bring positive changes to their lives. Despite his initial disinterest in the sport, Giannis gave it a shot, realizing that basketball might provide his family with much-needed support.

Giannis and his brother, Thanasis, both played and practiced basketball and their progress was very quick! Three years later, they were both playing for a Greek basketball team called Filathlitikos.

Basketball opened a new world for Giannis. He and his brother shared a single pair of sneakers, taking turns to play. Yet, even with limited resources, Giannis's athleticism stood out. It wasn't long before scouts and coaches noticed his potential. Grainy videos of Giannis's games made their way to international NBA scouts, catching the attention of Milwaukee Bucks' scouts. In 2013 he was drafted by the Bucks as the 15th overall pick! About this time he also gained Greek citizenship which enabled him to travel to the United States.

The journey to the NBA wasn't smooth. Giannis faced doubts and obstacles, but the Bucks saw something in him that others didn't. Milwaukee took a chance on this young man who didn't even know how to lift weights properly. Once on the court, Giannis's determination and hard work began to pay off. He embraced the spotlight with grace and humility, saving most of his earnings to support his family.

Giannis quickly gained attention for his incredible athleticism and versatility on the court. He earned the nickname "The Greek Freak" for his unique combination of height, agility, and skill. Despite his rising fame, Giannis stayed grounded and remembered his roots. He remained close to his family and continued to work hard to improve his game.

Giannis's rise in the NBA was marked by incredible achievements — back-to-back MVP awards, an NBA championship in 2021 — but what truly sets him apart is his unwavering humility. Despite fame and fortune, he remained grounded, never forgetting where he came from. Giannis and his brother established the AntetokounBros Academy, a charity aimed at providing opportunities to children who faced challenges similar to his own upbringing.

Giannis's story teaches us valuable lessons: to persevere when faced with adversity, to believe in ourselves even when the odds seem stacked against us, and to always stay humble no matter how high we rise. His journey from a tough beginning to becoming a global inspiration reminds us that with determination, hard work, and kindness, we can overcome challenges and reach for the stars, just like Giannis Antetokounmpo did.

LESSONS FROM GIANNIS'S JOURNEY:

- **Embrace Challenges as Opportunities:** Giannis faced many obstacles, but he didn't let them stop him. Instead of giving up, he used challenges as chances to learn and grow. When things are tough, remember that they can make you stronger.

- **Hard Work Pays Off:** Giannis practiced tirelessly to improve his basketball skills. He showed that hard work and dedication can turn your dreams into reality. Whether it's sports, school, or any other goal, putting in effort can lead to success.

- **Stay Humble:** Despite his fame, Giannis stayed down-to-earth. He remembered his humble beginnings and always treated others with respect. Being kind and humble can make you a better person and earn you the respect of those around you.

- **Help Others:** Giannis didn't forget where he came from. He used his success to create opportunities for kids facing challenges like he did. Giving back to your community and helping those in need can make a positive impact on the world.

- **Adapt to Change:** Giannis didn't plan on playing basketball, but he adapted when an opportunity came his way. Being open to new experiences and willing to try something different can lead you to unexpected successes.

- **Be Grateful:** Giannis never forgot his roots and the challenges he faced. Being grateful for what you have and the progress you make along the way can keep you grounded and appreciative of your journey.

LEON POWE

I'll put something out tomorrow. You'll know then.

- Leon Powe

Leon Powe was born on January 22, 1984, in Oakland, California. From the moment he took his first breath, his life was filled with challenges. Growing up in a rough neighborhood, he faced many difficulties, but his determination to rise above them would define his journey.

Leon's father left him when he was only two years old. He was raised by a single mother who worked hard to make ends meet. When he was seven years old, their family home burned down. Their family became homeless and was forced to live in homeless shelters, motels, and cars for several years! They moved more than 20 times in just 6 years. A lot of times, they would have nothing to eat. One time, their mother even got arrested for stealing groceries. Leon and his siblings were taken away by the California government and put into foster care.

Leon grew up in a very tough neighborhood in Oakland. Leon often had to take cover from the sound of gunshots ringing out. He would often see the tragic sight of drug dealers being shot right within his apartment complex. Leon has always had a good head on his shoulders. He could've become one of the drug dealers but he stayed on the right track and that paid off.

One time, Leon almost got involved with a robbery that could've put him in jail. His story might have been so different from what it is now. He was just a teenager and his friends were pressuring him to come along as they were on their way to rob someone. Leon went with them for a few blocks, he has never robbed anyone before. A voice inside his head kept telling him to turn around, it got so loud that he finally made up an excuse to leave and he ran home. The next day, he received news that his friends were all arrested for robbery! He could have been one of them! Leon realized he did the right thing and vowed to always stay on the right track.

Leon attended Oakland Technical High School, where his skills on the basketball court started to gain attention. With Leon on the team, Oakland Tech won the CIF Oakland Section Championship and made it to the CIF State Championships in 2002 and 2003. He was given important awards like being a first-team Parade All-American and the Gatorade California Player of the Year in his senior year of high school. He was really good, so he got picked to play in the McDonald's All-American game. He was so amazing that his school, Oakland Tech, decided to retire his jersey number, and he was the first athlete from the school to get this honor.

Life outside the gymnasium was still tough, though. His mother died when he was in his senior year which took a toll on Leon. Gang violence and negative influences were a constant presence. Leon had to make difficult choices and stay focused on his goals, despite the distractions around him.

Leon's dedication paid off, and he earned a scholarship to the University of California, Berkeley. College life brought new challenges, both academically and athletically. Balancing his studies and basketball was no easy feat, but Leon knew that education was his ticket to a better future. He showed that with hard work and perseverance, anyone could overcome obstacles.

Leon's college basketball career was marked by impressive performances and incredible determination. He played with the California Golden Bears, earning recognition as one of the top college players in the country. His hard-nosed playing style and indomitable spirit made him a fan favorite.

In 2006, Leon's dreams came true when he was selected in the second round of the NBA Draft by the Denver Nuggets and was quickly traded to the Boston Celtics. Playing alongside legends like Paul Pierce, Kevin Garnett, and Ray Allen, Leon became an integral part of the Celtics' resurgence. His tireless work ethic, especially on the defensive end, earned him respect throughout the league.

However, the challenges didn't stop. Injuries continued to plague Leon throughout his NBA career. He faced multiple surgeries and grueling rehabilitation processes.

Each time, he fought back, refusing to let setbacks define him. His ability to rebound from adversity became one of his greatest strengths.

Leon's resilience reached its peak during the 2008 NBA Finals. The Celtics faced the Los Angeles Lakers in a fierce battle for the championship. In Game 2, Leon's tenacity shone brightly as he scored 21 points and grabbed 7 rebounds, helping the Celtics secure a crucial victory. His performance became an inspiration to everyone watching.

Leon's playing career eventually came to an end due to the toll of injuries but his journey didn't stop there. He turned his attention to mentoring and coaching young players, passing on the lessons he had learned through his own struggles. He showed that while basketball was a significant part of his life, the values of hard work, determination, and resilience were what truly defined him.

Leon Powe's journey is a testament to the power of perseverance. His life story teaches us that no matter where we come from or what challenges we face, we can overcome them through dedication and a never-give-up attitude. Leon's story encourages us to believe in ourselves, to embrace challenges as opportunities for growth, and to never lose sight of our dreams.

Leon Powe's legacy lives on in the hearts of those he inspired. His story continues to motivate young athletes, reminding them that success is born from hard work and determination. journey from a humble beginning to the heights of the NBA serves as a beacon of hope for all who face challenges on their path to greatness.

LESSONS FROM LEON'S JOURNEY:

- **Create a Better Future:** From his early days in a tough neighborhood to witnessing violence and homelessness, Leon's life could have taken a very different path. He refused to let his circumstances define him. He used basketball as a way to escape his challenges and create a better future for himself.

- **Resilience:** Leon's determination was put to the test when he suffered injuries that could have ended his basketball dreams. Instead of giving up, he tackled rehabilitation with unwavering persistence. His ability to rebound from setbacks demonstrates the importance of resilience. Life is full of ups and downs, but it's our response to challenges that truly matters.

- **Discipline and Commitment:** Leon's success wasn't handed to him; he earned it through hard work and dedication. He balanced his studies and sports, showing that education is just as important as talent. This reminds us that excellence requires discipline and a commitment to both our passions and our responsibilities.

- **Making Good Choices:** The lesson from Leon's journey also extends to making choices. Growing up amidst negativity and distractions, he made choices that aligned with his dreams. By staying focused and surrounding himself with positive influences, he demonstrated that our decisions shape our paths. He never gave in to bad peer pressure.

- **Giving Back:** Leon's story emphasizes the importance of giving back. After his playing career, he turned to coaching and mentoring, using his experiences to inspire and guide young athletes. This reminds us that as we achieve our goals, it's our duty to support others on their journeys too.

BEN MCLEMORE

> "It doesn't matter what life deals you, play the cards the best way you can." - **Ben McLemore**

Ben's journey from a small town to the bright lights of the NBA is a story of determination, perseverance, and the will to overcome obstacles. In this chapter, we will delve into the life of Ben McLemore, exploring the challenges he faced and the lessons he learned along the way.

Ben McLemore's story begins in St. Louis, Missouri. He is the fourth of five children and comes from a very tight-knit family. Unfortunately, the whole family underwent extreme poverty that resulted in frequent hunger. They also experienced neighborhood violence and violence involving family. His mother had to work hard to support the family. It motivated Ben to work harder to fight difficulties in life and succeed.

Ben had to share one bed with his siblings and oftentimes, they would go to bed hungry. He has experienced hunger pains so bad that he would eventually feel mad or upset and then throw tantrums because of the extreme hunger.

Ben and his family have also relied on candles when the electricity was turned off. They would turn on the stove and haul a kerosene heater to the middle of the room to stay warm. All the family members would huddle in the room, covered in layers of clothing and blankets, sometimes able to see their own breath in the chilled winter air.

As Ben grew older, his basketball skills flourished. He joined the Wellston high school team and quickly became a star player. However, his journey wasn't without setbacks. During his junior year, he faced academic struggles that made him ineligible to play. This was a turning point. Ben realized that excelling in the classroom was just as important as on the court. With hard work and support from teachers and mentors, he overcame his academic challenges and returned stronger than ever.

When he was 15 years old, Ben's older brother was arrested and imprisoned. Ben was worried about being the man of the house. To him, basketball was so much easier to handle compared to all these challenges going on in his household. His brother's situation motivated him to excel on the court and compete every night. He even led Wellston High School to the Missouri State semifinals in 2010!

After high school, Ben's dreams led him to the University of Kansas, a renowned college basketball program. But here too, challenges awaited. The NCAA (National Collegiate Athletic Association) questioned his eligibility due to having attended multiple schools, making his transcript look unclear. Ben faced the possibility of not being able to play college basketball. With unwavering determination, he fought for his chance to shine on the court and they allowed him to join practices in the beginning before they finally let him play games. He ended up being the best scorer among all the new players in the conference. He used his excellent skills and ability to shoot from far away to really beat the other teams. This experience taught him the importance of perseverance and standing up for what is right.

McLemore got a special title as an All-American, and he was a big help in making his team, the Jayhawks, win the Big 12 championship. After Kansas' games in the NCAA tournament were done, he decided to join the NBA draft.

In 2013, Ben's hard work paid off when he was selected in the NBA Draft. He joined the Sacramento Kings, entering the big leagues of professional basketball. However, the transition wasn't smooth. Ben faced intense competition and struggled to find his footing in the NBA. He learned that success at the highest level requires continuous effort and adaptability.

Despite the challenges, Ben refused to give up. He continued to work hard and improve his skills. His determination paid off when he became a valuable player for the Kings. He faced injuries and tough losses, but each setback only fueled his desire to succeed. Ben's story teaches us that setbacks are temporary, and with perseverance, we can overcome any obstacle.

Today, Ben is not just a basketball player but also an inspiration. He uses his platform to give back to his community and support children facing challenges similar to his own. His journey reminds us that no matter where we come from, with the right mindset and hard work, we can achieve our dreams.

Ben's story is an inspiring one, showing us that with the right mindset and a heart full of determination, anything is possible. As we face our own challenges, let his journey serve as a guiding light, reminding us that we too can rise above obstacles and reach for the stars.

LESSONS FROM BEN'S JOURNEY:

- **Hard Work Pays Off**: Ben's journey shows that consistent effort and dedication can turn dreams into reality.

- **Adversity is an Opportunity**: Challenges are stepping stones, not roadblocks. Ben's ability to turn adversity into strength is a lesson for us all.

- **Stay True to Yourself**: Ben stayed true to his passion for basketball while also valuing education. This balance helped him overcome obstacles on and off the court.

- **Help Others Along the Way:** Ben's commitment to giving back teaches us the importance of supporting those facing challenges similar to our own.

- **Never Give Up:** Ben's persistence, even in the face of setbacks, is a reminder that success often requires pushing through tough times.

BEN WALLACE

> "The bigger your dreams are, the less your fall is."
> **- Ben Wallace**

In the world of basketball, there are some players who stand out not just because of their skills on the court, but also because of the challenges they've overcome. One such player is Ben Wallace. Born on September 10, 1974, in White Hall, Alabama, Ben's journey from a small town to becoming a basketball legend is nothing short of inspiring. This book will take you on a journey through Ben Wallace's life, focusing on his challenges and struggles, and how he turned them into stepping stones to success.

Ben Wallace grew up in a small town where life wasn't always easy. His family didn't have a lot of money and they had a lot of mouths to feed. Ben is the 11th out of 12 children in the Wallace household and is the youngest of 8 brothers. Even as a young boy, Ben showed an interest in sports, particularly basketball. He loved playing with his brothers in the neighborhood, using makeshift hoops and worn-out basketballs. The Wallace kids helped out at nearby pecan farms to make money. With some of the money they earned, they got a basketball hoop for their house. Despite not having the fanciest equipment, Ben's passion for the game shone brightly.

As the youngest of all the brothers, Ben was able to develop his on-court speed when they played pick-up games. He had to play tough and chase after all the loose balls as his brothers wouldn't pass him the ball. He explained in Sports Illustrated, *"Since I was the younger brother, I understood they wouldn't give me the ball. If I wanted to touch it, I had to take it away, catch a rebound, or prevent the ball from going out of bounds."*

When Ben was ready to attend high school, he decided to try out for his school's basketball team. But there was a problem – he was considered too short to play the game at a high level. Coaches and even some of his friends doubted his abilities because of his height. However, Ben didn't let their doubts bring him down. He worked twice as hard to prove that height doesn't determine a player's worth. His determination paid off, and he not only made the team but also became a key player.

While attending Central High School in Hayneville, Ben achieved honors in basketball, football, and baseball. In the summer before his junior year in high school, he learned about a basketball camp organized by his hero, Charles Oakley from the Chicago Bulls. The camp was in York, Alabama, which was 60 miles away from his home. To be able to afford the $50 fee for the camp, Ben gave haircuts for three dollars each. Oakley was very impressed by his hard work and kept in touch as Ben's career progressed.

Despite his impressive record in high school, Ben didn't receive any college scholarship offers. Many colleges didn't think he had what it took to succeed in the competitive world of college basketball. But Ben didn't give up. He attended a small community college in Cleveland for 2 years. He didn't waste the opportunity he got by going to that college and impressed everybody with his defensive basketball skills as he averaged 17 rebounds and 7 blocked shots per game! He used this rejection as motivation to work even harder, proving that sometimes, a setback can be a setup for a comeback.

Remember Ben's idol Charles Oakley? He did keep in touch with Ben and recommended Ben attend his alma mater Virginia Union University, so Ben applied and got in. There, Ben became a Division II All-American first–team honors as he led the team to the Final Four championship games in Division II college basketball.

Again, in spite of Ben's impressive performance at Virginia Union, not many professional scouts knew about him or were interested. They still thought he was not tall enough for the NBA. After he finished his studies in criminal justice at Virginia Union in 1996, Wallace still didn't get picked in the NBA draft. Many people thought his basketball journey was over. However, Ben wasn't about to let a setback define him. He continued to work on his skills and fitness, never losing sight of his dream to play in the NBA.

Eventually, Ben's hard work paid off. He was signed as an undrafted free agent by the Washington Wizards, marking the beginning of his NBA career. He almost got cut during training camp but ended up getting a spot as a backup forward. In his first year, he only played in 34 games. But in the following year, Ben started to show his skills more and got to play more often. The fans really liked him especially because of how hard he worked on defense, grabbing rebounds, and blocking shots.

His incredible defensive skills and determination caught the attention of the Detroit Pistons, who traded for him. Ben became the heart and soul of the Pistons, known for his amazing shot-blocking, rebounding, and defensive plays. He was even nominated for the MVP award. He proved that hard work, passion, and dedication can make up for any challenges one faces.

One of Ben's biggest achievements came in the 2001-2002 NBA season when he was named the NBA Defensive Player of the Year, which he won again two more times. He became only the fourth player in history, and probably the first who was shorter than six feet ten inches, to be the best in the league at both getting rebounds and blocking shots.

The Pistons, led by Ben's defensive prowess, made it to the NBA championship during the 2003 - 2004 season. Ben has won so many awards since then. This victory wasn't just about the trophy or awards; it was about showing the world that a team can overcome adversity and challenges to become champions. Ben's journey from being undrafted to becoming an NBA champion was an inspiration to everyone who heard his story.

Ben Wallace's journey from a small town to the NBA is a testament to the power of perseverance, resilience, and self-belief. He showed that challenges are opportunities in disguise, and with the right attitude, anyone can overcome them. Ben's story continues to inspire young and old alike, reminding us that no dream is too big if we're willing to work for it. So, remember Ben's journey whenever you face challenges, and let it inspire you to keep pushing forward and never give up.

LESSONS FROM BEN'S JOURNEY:

- **Resilience and Determination:** Ben's journey teaches us that setbacks and obstacles are opportunities for growth. He didn't let doubts, rejections, or setbacks deter him. Instead, he used them as stepping stones to improve and prove his worth.

- **Embrace Differences:** Despite being initially dismissed due to his height, Ben proved that one's potential is not limited by physical attributes. He teaches us to embrace our differences and turn them into strengths.

- **Hard Work Pays Off:** Ben's tireless work ethic is a reminder that hard work and dedication are the keys to success. He didn't rely solely on talent; he consistently honed his skills, both on and off the court, to become a dominant force.

- **Turn Setbacks into Comebacks:** Ben's rejection from college scholarships and going undrafted could have been endpoints, but he used them as motivation to work even harder. His story emphasizes that setbacks can be setups for comebacks.

- **Keep Pursuing Dreams:** Ben's tenacity to pursue his dream of playing in the NBA, despite numerous challenges, is a testament to the importance of unwavering determination in achieving your aspirations.

CONCLUSION

As we wrap up the pages of "Amazing Basketball Stories for Kids," I, Leigh Jordyn, want to give you a big high-five, and a big thank you from the bottom of my heart, for being part of this exciting journey. I hope you've had a slam-dunk time reading these stories!

From buzzer-beating shots to friendships that make your heart smile, these stories are like a warm hug from basketball itself. Remember, it's not just about the game; it's about trying your best, never giving up, and cheering on your teammates.

As you turn the final pages, I hope you've not only had fun but also learned some cool stuff — like how teamwork can make dreams work, and how practicing hard can turn you into a superstar both on and off the court.

Just like the players in these stories, you have your own special talents that make you shine. Whether it's in sports, school, or being a great friend, you're a champion in your own way!

So, keep the high-fives going, spread kindness like confetti, and keep these lessons close to your heart. They are like a compass that will guide you as you grow and discover the amazing things you can achieve. As you go forward, shoot for the stars and dribble through challenges with a big smile.

Thanks for joining me in the game of stories. You're a true MVP, and your adventure is just getting started!

THANK YOU

Dear Young Reader and Parents,

I want to express my deepest gratitude for choosing my book among the many options out there. As you've journeyed through its pages, I can't thank you enough for your time and trust.

Before your next reading journey, could I ask a small favor? Would you consider sharing your thoughts in a review? For independent authors like myself, your feedback is invaluable and the easiest way to show support. It's through your insights that I can keep crafting books that resonate with you and bring the results you seek. Your words would mean everything to me.

With heartfelt thanks,

Leigh Jordyn

REFERENCES

1. Murphy, D. (2017b, October 3). 21 people Who made LeBron James the man he is today. Bleacher Report. https://bleacherreport.com/articles/1876553-21-people-who-made-lebron-james-the-man-he-is-today

2. LeBron James Biography for Kids. (n.d.-b). https://www.ducksters.com/sports/lebron_james. php#:~:text=LeBron%20James%20was%20 born%20in,and%20had%20a%20tough%20time

3. Param, A. (2023). LeBron James Childhood: Where is King James from? Sportsmanor. https:// sportsmanor.com/nba-lebron-james-childhood-where-is-king-james-from/

4. Michael Jordan Biography - life, family, children, story, death, history, wife, school, mother, young. (n.d.). https://www.notablebiographies.com/Jo-Ki/ Jordan-Michael.html

5. LeSueur, B. (2021). The History of Michael Jordan for Kids. Commonlit. https://www.commonlit.org/en/texts/the-history-of-michael-jordan-for-kids

6. Michael Jordan's Biography - 23jordan.com - A Michael Jordan Tribute. (n.d.). https://www.23jordan.com/bio

7. Say, J. (2020, July 25). 27 Best Larry Bird Quotes on Life (WINNING). Gracious Quotes. https://graciousquotes.com/larry-bird/

8. Wikipedia contributors. (2002). Larry Bird. Wikipedia. https://en.wikipedia.org/wiki/Larry_Bird#

9. Who is Larry Bird? Everything You Need to Know. (n.d.). https://www.thefamouspeople.com/profiles/larry-bird-8527.php

10. SportyTell. (2020). Larry Bird Biography, Childhood, career, life, facts. SportyTell. https://sportytell.com/biography/larry-bird-biography-childhood-career-life-facts/

11. Schwantes, M. (2021, January 5). 15 Kobe Bryant quotes from his legendary career that will inspire you. Inc.com. https://www.inc.com/marcel-schwantes/15-kobe-bryant-quotes-from-his-legendary-career-that-will-inspire-you.

html#:~:text=%22Once%20you%20know%20
what%20failure,It%20will%20not%20
process%20failure

12.   Kobe Bryant Biography for Kids. (n.d.). https://
www.ducksters.com/sports/kobe_bryant.php

13.   LakersNation.com. (2023, February 24). Kobe
Bryant Biography | Early Life, Career & Stats |
Lakers Nation. Lakers Nation. https://lakersnation.
com/kobe-bryant-biography-life-lakers-career-and-
legacy/#google_vignette

14.   Krishnamurthy, A. (2021, September 28).
Kobe Bryant Shares Motivational Story About His
Childhood Struggles: "I Grew Up In Italy With No
Friends." Yardbarker. https://www.yardbarker.com/
nba/articles/kobe_bryant_shares_motivational_
story_about_his_childhood_struggles_i_grew_up_
in_italy_with_no_friends/s1_16751_35991317

15.   Gavin Newsham. (2022, January 8). How
growing up in Italy for 7 years turned Kobe
Bryant into a star. New York Post. https://nypost.
com/2022/01/08/how-kobe-bryants-childhood-in-
italy-turned-him-into-a-star/

16.   Param, A. (2022). Kevin Durant's childhood
and how he started his NBA career. Sportsmanor.

https://sportsmanor.com/kevin-durant-childhood-and-how-he-started-his-nba-career

17. Castillo, J. (2022). The Rise Of Kevin Durant: From Humble Beginnings To NBA Stardom. https://bashabearsbasketball.com/the-rise-of-kevin-durant-from-humble-beginnings-to-nba-stardom

18. Kevin Durant Biography: NBA basketball player. (n.d.). https://www.ducksters.com/sports/kevin_durant.php

19. EssentiallySports. (n.d.). EssentiallySports | The Fan's Perspective. https://www.essentiallysports.com/

20. Johnson, J. D. (2022, September 23). Best Kevin Durant quotes [2023 updated]. TheChampLair. https://thechamplair.com/basketball/kevin-durant-quotes/

21. Familytron, & Emma. (2023). Kevin Durant. Familytron. https://familytron.com/kevin-durant/

22. Frey, T. (2023, May 3). Jimmy Butler Biography: From Being Kicked Out Of Home At 13 Years Old To Becoming A True NBA Star. Fadeaway World. https://fadeawayworld.net/jimmy-butler-biography-from-being-kicked-out-of-home-at-13-years-old-to-becoming-a-true-nba-star

23. David. (n.d.). Jimmy Butler's emotional story: From homeless teenager to NBA All-Star. Ballislife LLC. https://ballislife.com/jimmy-butlers-emotional-story-from-homeless-teenager-to-nba-all-star/

24. Bucher, R. (2017, October 3). Left alone, Jimmy Butler has found NBA stardom one new family member at a time. Bleacher Report. https://bleacherreport.com/articles/2359572-left-alone-jimmy-butler-has-found-nba-stardom-one-new-family-member-at-a-time

25. Shoe Palace. (2023, May 8). The Life Of Jimmy Butler. https://www.shoepalace.com/blogs/all/the-life-of-jimmy-butler

26. Wikipedia contributors. (2023). Jimmy Butler. Wikipedia. https://en.wikipedia.org/wiki/Jimmy_Butler

27. Wikipedia contributors. (2023). Jimmy Butler. Wikipedia. https://en.wikipedia.org/wiki/Jimmy_Butler

28. Caron Butler biography and stats. (n.d.). https://caronbutler.com/biography-stats

29. Wikipedia contributors. (2023a). Caron Butler. Wikipedia. https://en.wikipedia.org/wiki/Caron_Butler

30. Odhiambo, A. (2022, September 28). Caron Butler journey from a troubled childhood to the NBA. Latest Sports News Africa ⎮ Latest Sports Results. https://sportsleo.com/news/2022/09/caron-butler-journey-from-a-troubled-childhood-to-the-nba/

31. Griffin, C. (2018). The Caron Butler Story. All Things Hoops. https://www.allthingshoops.com/caron-butler-story/

32. Wallin, E. (2023). 60 Famous Dwyane Wade quotes about hard work. Wealthy Gorilla. https://wealthygorilla.com/dwyane-wade-quotes/

33. Wikipedia contributors. (2023b). Dwyane Wade. Wikipedia. https://en.wikipedia.org/wiki/Dwyane_Wade

34. Augustyn, A. (2023, August 16). Dwyane Wade ⎮ Biography, Statistics, & Facts. Encyclopedia Britannica. https://www.britannica.com/biography/Dwyane-Wade

35. Wallin, E. (2023b). 60 Famous Dwyane Wade quotes about hard work. Wealthy Gorilla. https://wealthygorilla.com/dwyane-wade-quotes/

36. TOP 25 QUOTES BY JEREMY LIN (of 75) ⎮ A-Z Quotes. (n.d.). A-Z Quotes. https://www.azquotes.com/author/8877-Jeremy_Lin

37. Jeremy Lin. (2023, March 7). Biography. https://www.biography.com/athletes/jeremy-lin

38. Wikipedia contributors. (2009). Jeremy Lin. Wikipedia. https://en.wikipedia.org/wiki/Jeremy_Lin

39. Jeremy Lin. (n.d.). Britannica Kids. https://kids.britannica.com/students/article/Jeremy-Lin/634221

40. Moraitis, M. (2017, September 25). Jeremy Lin's Story a Blueprint for Why You Should Never Give Up on a Dream. Bleacher Report. https://bleacherreport.com/articles/1194297-jeremy-lins-story-a-blueprint-for-why-you-should-never-give-up-on-a-dream

41. Allen Iverson Quotes. (n.d.). Brainy Quotes. https://www.brainyquote.com/authors/allen-iverson-quotes

42. Allen Iverson. (2023, March 7). Biography. https://www.biography.com/athletes/allen-iverson

43. IMDb. (n.d.). Allen Iverson. IMDb. https://www.imdb.com/name/nm1132515/bio/

44. Wikipedia contributors. (2003). Allen Iverson. Wikipedia. https://en.wikipedia.org/wiki/Allen_Iverson

45. 247Sports. (n.d.). Derrick Rose quotes. https://247sports.com/Player/Derrick-Rose-63103/Quotes/

46. Wikipedia contributors. (2023d). Derrick Rose. Wikipedia. https://en.wikipedia.org/wiki/Derrick_Rose

47. Derrick Rose. (2023, March 7). Biography. https://www.biography.com/athlete/derrick-rose

48. The Editors of Encyclopaedia Britannica. (2004, December 3). Allen Iverson | Biography, Stats, & Facts. Encyclopedia Britannica. https://www.britannica.com/biography/Allen-Iverson

49. Giannis Antetokounmpo Quotes. (n.d.). Brainy Quotes. https://www.brainyquote.com/authors/giannis-antetokounmpo-quotes

50. Tikkanen, A. (2023, August 19). Giannis Antetokounmpo | Height, Brothers, Stats, & Milwaukee Bucks. Encyclopedia Britannica. https://www.britannica.com/biography/Giannis-Antetokounmpo

51. Binner, A. (2023, June 27). Giannis Antetokounmpo: From poverty in Greece to NBA's most lucrative player. Olympics.com. https://

olympics.com/en/news/giannis-antetokounmpo-
nba-milwaukee-bucks-greece

52.   Wikipedia   contributors.   (2023e).   Giannis
Antetokounmpo.   Wikipedia.   https://en.wikipedia.
org/wiki/Giannis_Antetokounmpo

53.   yrics-quotes-status.com.   (n.d.).   I   told   coach
to put him back in. One foot, no foot, zero foot.
Doesn't matter. http://bdir.in/quotes. https://etc.
bdir.in/quotes/view/NDUyNTg3

54.   Okanes, J. (2018, October). Leon Powe's Success
Story Continues In Boston. Inside the Lair. https://
calbears.com/news/2018/10/4/inside-the-lair-leon-
powes-success-story-continues-in-boston

55.   Wikipedia contributors. (2023b). Leon Powe.
Wikipedia.   https://en.wikipedia.org/wiki/Leon_
Powe#Regular_season

56.   Kessler, M. (2016, December 9). Former NBA
Player Leon Powe Has Home In Celtics Front Office
I Only A Game. WBUR.org. https://www.wbur.org/
onlyagame/2016/12/09/leon-powe-nba-celtics

57.   Wikipedia contributors. (2023f). Ben McLemore.
Wikipedia.   https://en.wikipedia.org/wiki/Ben_
McLemore

58. Sportskeeda. (2023, April 15). Ben McLemore News, Biography, NBA Records, Stats & Facts. https://www.sportskeeda.com/basketball/ben-mclemore

59. O'Brien, D. (2017, August 4). Crib-to-Draft timeline of NBA draft prospect Ben McLemore's rise to NBA draft. Bleacher Report. https://bleacherreport.com/articles/1676009-crib-to-draft-timeline-of-nba-draft-prospect-ben-mclemores-rise-to-nba-draft

60. Ben Wallace Quotes. (n.d.). Brainy Quote. https://www.brainyquote.com/authors/ben-wallace-quotes

61. Wikipedia contributors. (2023c). Ben Wallace (basketball). Wikipedia. https://en.wikipedia.org/wiki/Ben_Wallace_(basketball)

62. Ben Wallace Biography. (n.d.). https://biography.jrank.org/pages/2884/Wallace-Ben.html

63. Ben Wallace Biography - life, children, name, history, school, son, born, college, tall, time - Newsmakers Cumulation. (n.d.). https://www.notablebiographies.com/newsmakers2/2004-Q-Z/Wallace-Ben.html

18831103R00076